Wail Words

Seleka Behrs

BookLeaf Publishing

India | USA | UK

Presentation by *BookLeaf Publishing*

Web: www.bookleafpub.com

E-mail: info@bookleafpub.com

ISBN: 9789360946609

First edition 2024

Dedicated to every childless mother and motherless child, and those who have lost themselves in grief, in love, or in unrequited yearning for a different timeline.

ACKNOWLEDGEMENT

With sincerest gratitude for Dominic Crooks, Johnna Sims, Sharin Joy Price, and all who have encouraged me along the way.

PREFACE

Seleka Behrs surfs emotions; she swims in them. These deep waters are where she plays freely as a whale. She is not afraid of sadness, anger, melancholy, fear, regret, or confusion. The deep flow currents carry us into darkness far away from land, and it's helpful to have guidance on the journey back to the shores of contentment, joy, and love. She is a natural guide, following the flow, searching for sunlight at the surface, catching her breath again and again. Seleka's voice wails to other whales, letting them know they are not alone in the vastness of the void.

Arctic Mother

I am an arctic mother
Made of bear claws and wolf jaws
Of fox furs and rabbit curves
Dancing under auroral paintings of Night Sky

I am an arctic mother
Made of cool resilience and warm passions
Of piercing silences and deep reverence
Singing by the water paths of Summer Wind

I am an arctic mother
Made of loose pragmatism and complex
optimism
Of tender wilderness and chaotic kinderness
Playing with the fabric phases of Mother Time

I am Her arctic daughter
Made of solid stardust and earthen cords
Of interlaced magnetism and watery currents
Holding important keys to seasons of change

Deep Waters

I walk through the graveyard of past ambitions
With hushed reverence for the dead versions of
desires
They haunt spaces between sleep and awake
As though I could revive them in my dreams

I dance through the waves of my last recitals
With rushed feet I leap from the grains of
sand-barred solace
My rhythm paces faster than the tides can raise
me
As though I could run from the ebb into the flow

There's nothing holding me except gravity
Nothing supporting me except levity
I cry out for kindness in community
Only to fall harshly in the silent storms

I tear through the torrents of creative
dissolutions
With calloused hands I pick through the
deadwood
My art is my life and beauty is an anchor
As though without it, I would be lost, never seen

I sing with the whispers of wind across a horizon
With passionate emotions sourced from deep
reflections
Any force of my will has been overridden by
acceptance
As though every improvisation surfaces from
grace

I am held in deep waters and supported by
currents
With undulating rhythms pulling and pulsing
through dreams
My slumber is full of chaos that holds an
awakened view
As though the separation between worlds is a
thin veil

Holding the Pause

This gratitude outweighs the heartache.
Shattered shell and darkened taste.
Buried. Protected. Mourning.
Grief yields a gravity that holds me still.
I am an anchored witness to the beauty of this
moment.
Sunlight dancing in rhythms of sensory
vibration.
Life's pulse reflected in the pauses of my breath.
Listening to these heartbreaks and kissing my
sleeve.
I've worn this. I'm worn. I have warned.
I'm soft. I'm transparent. I'm loved.
In the swirled breath of the present wind
I am carried. I am supported. I'm safe.
My fears are valid. I am not in control.
My faith is valid. I am not in control.
I am alive in this chaos of change.
Out with the old breath in with the new heir.
Tumbled from raw to shine.
Kissed by dirt, these roots I grew.
I have paws to play in the earth.
I pause to live warmly under the sun.
Belly up. Chest full. Gaze wide.

Late Brother

5

Mother Earth receives a
body as a gift for her
contribution

Father Time ceases a
totalitarian reign over his
next phase

Earthly Mother mourns the
separation of mortal bounds
of familial parentage

Releasing her precious child to the
expansive timelessness
of his pure spiritual bliss

Energetic bonds formed and
rearranged, silently severed
with one last breath

Sun's Raise

Celebrate the sun
While living below the blue
Winds of change swirl and guide
Grief-gratitude cycles anew
Clouds in the sky
Cry rivers of roaring tears
Sourced from the traumas
Of unreasoned expectations
And unreliable fears
Of many many years

Loss and Gain
Ebb and Flow
Existing on the down low
Step outside
Take deep breaths
High on life
Forward one more step

Leave the house twice a month for supplies
Spend lots of time outside
Have no visitors, hear no laughter
Lose track of a day, at least once a week
Get lots and lots and lots of sleep
Over-commit to virtual hangouts

Under-deliver, halt productivity

Par for the course
No alarms
No surprises
Letting go is not the same as acceptance
Until gratitude blows away the grief
Sit still in the silence of now
And discover the quiet's loud

Accept the exceptions
And dance in the mystery
Of these unfolding circumstances
Hope is the dazzling water of life
While living below the blue
Celebrating the sun

My Toxic Traits

My toxic trait is
not believing you love me
if I smell a whiff of malice
or a hint of indifference

I gag on the smell of your
ignorant jealousies

I cannot hide my disgust

My toxic trait is
giving you credit for your potential

when you tax my forgiveness
every time we interact in private

I wince at the pain of
your last friendly punch

I cannot ignore my pride

My toxic trait is
offering the benefit of the doubt

to pirates and liars in costumes

who withdraw more than they deposit

I cannot abide my stupor

Devotion of Miss Understanding

Devotion purifies the space
to make room for the
silent rhythms to be heard
and the patterns to be seen

The holy circle of semi-permanence
is constantly holding and letting go
before it detaches yearnings of the mind
and breathes life into the heart of all matter

You can want to become a better person
without thinking you are a bad person
Nature is balancing itself one phase at a time
moving frequency into constancy

Sun shining on cold winter days
can be confusing and disorienting
Maybe that is why I am misunderstood
in this cold dark world

Imperceptible growth is happening
in the down time, the sadness, the darkness
Perceptible growth comes after the seed
has been fully nourished and the time is right

Arguments cease when awareness comes
that lower vibration is a necessary state
not a demeaning dementor of punishment
separated from the whole of the experience

Holistic mindfulness is incomplete
if it disconnects or bypasses the sum
of day and night respectively paced
through darkness and light

Cycles of seasons compressed
into moments of ancient remembrance
The sun's spontaneous revival
wakes always on time

Caught & Quartered

There you are, I caught you
Spinning tales and turning tail

Like a predator you stalk
Preying with positive self-talk

Nothing like a sharp-voiced soothsayer
Spending money on nothing that's for sale

Living life under the radar; under the fold; under
the veil
Proving nothing can be sacred amidst your
betrayal

There you are, illuminated by the weak
of your incessant need to speak.

These windows fog when compliments
beseeched
In your presence, hope cowers coldly, just out of
reach

Duplicitous ramblings, overzealous hugs, amidst
promises of pity

I caught you sneaking shadows into Rainbow's
morning tea

Fuck you for everything and thank you for the
fish
I learned how to spot your piracy culture - and I
know where you live

Let's avoid this dramatic conversation amiss
Go on, now. Good day. I said, "GOOD DAY!"
No kiss.

The Castle is the Temple

You've never seen me with perimeter walls.
I've been an unprotected castle
with high turrets and deep dungeons.
My moat has been easy to cross,
deliberately shallow,
holding no aggressive reptiles.

I've been guarded by the wind
and sheltered by flowers.
Golden light pierces my windows
and falls on plush rugs and fine linens.

"Come in and get comfortable!"
Happily, I share the stores of these cupboards,
locks open and doors ajar.

I've been vulnerable to thieves
and foolish to keep that openness
after attackers took everything,
save my stone.

They didn't break me.
I've not been conquered.
I'm exhausted from the fight
to regain strength.

It is time to build walls.
Not to become a debtor's prison.

I create protection for the sacred.
For I am no longer standing as a castle,
I am a temple.

Nothing has changed, except everything.
I house a sanctity that can only thrive
With wisdom earned and boundaries enforced.

The neighbors coming to pillage
Meet a full moat hosting aggressive reptiles
After they have broken through the barriers
Long overdue.

They will bow in reverence
For the life and love protected
Behind these stone barriers
Holding peaceful relations

The FireBird Bound

The red dragon dies
So the firebird can soar high
In its phoenix form

Birthed from a small egg
Woke in a loud combustion
Of Source and Mother

Bars bind the small bird
Spreading wings to fly
With nowhere to go

It screeches and blows fire
At the impenetrably
Cold and rigid metal

Frustrated and tired
It curls into a spiral
And weeps intensely

Tears pooling as lakes
Dousing its inner fire
To quiet darkness

Declare Interdependence

Within we are without separation
Interlocking networks of emotions
Interweaving vines of thoughts when
Interdependence wins the world

And yet we have these
fiercely independent rebellions
Dividing our individual perspectives
and rewarding our missed alignments

Fear creates cliques of lazy thoughts
crusted with futile examinations
Which become the isolated
distance between the hearts

Fenced

I've heard it is a big no-no
All or nothing: popular way to go
But whoa
No yard's grass is greener than yours
Its shade equally as dark in the moors
Closed doors
Nothing as easy as it seems
Precariously perched upon high beams
Extremes
The preference is to be the bridge
Be sacred connection from ridge to ridge
Courage
Beneath wrestling angst of turmoil
True inner peace comes from nourished soil
Uncoil
The way to be the source of hope
The pattern unknots the end of the rope
World scope
Love beats true, wise, sacred, and kind
Travel passed the confines of the mind
You'll find
A dearest bond with all alive
Serves constant protection in the hive
We thrive

Breath in the Heart

I see through because I want to see you
Your soft hands are welcome to touch mine
This embrace we share heals our hearts
Accepting all that is between and within us
All of your phases are whole
And you deserve this love
Even on the dampest and darkest night
Of your winter new moon
You can accept this love lighting your way home
Down in the deepest levels of your ocean
I love you there, too
Whales of a kindred song
You heard me from miles away
I hear your echo in the currents
Welcoming your vocal guidance
Feeling safe in every cell
I swim the channel's passage to home
The pain you thought was love
Has caused enough suffering
Unmask your internal uniqueness
Listen to your innermost feelings
Detangle the ties twisted by sour love
Be what love truly means
Intentionally caring for yourself, for us
Enacting healthy boundaries

Is what comes next in the journey
Of self-exploration in confident admiration
Because you are listening to
The Call
Of your heart's song
I found you
You found us
We found love
Exchanges of affection
Organically grow with conscious curiosity
There is no pedestal here
We see eye to eye
Witnessing reflections of seers
Discovering their truest selves
Our kindred connection revealed
By each present moment of sync

Saintly Valentine

They show me cheesy displays of affection
Every day
They work intense hours to provide
the most comfortable and stable life
I have ever known
They massage me with their tired hands
until they fall asleep at night
and often again in the morning
Making love with me is never far from their
mind
They dance with me for the sole purpose
of conjuring a smile
They literally live to see me smile, hear my
giggle
and watch my eyes light from inner joy
They hear me - really listening to what I say,
how I say it
and what I mean between the lines
They encourage me to be creative and
expressive
in every way that interests my soul
They cheer me on towards accomplishing ANY
goal I imagine
and they don't get upset when I hop from one
goal to another

They delight in my nature, as a butterfly or bee
hops from flower to flower
They see me, no matter my shape or size, as a
beautifully sexy
attractive being
They hold me when I cry and lift my spirits
when thoughts are too heavy
to carry alone
They never guilt me or manipulate my emotions
to get what they want
They remain curious about what makes me tick
They offer me the benefit of the doubt and
opportunity to explain
Sweet romanticism exists at the core of our
relationship
and I reciprocate all that I possibly can to show
them love in their way
We catch each other falling in love again and
again and again

Of This

We are all keepers of the light
The light of consciousness
The light of love
The light of kindness
The light of truth

We are all witnesses to the darkness
The darkness of isolation
The darkness of rejection
The darkness of cruelty
The darkness of lies

We have the capacity to shift
The shift of cooperation
The shift of abundance
The shift of equanimity
The shift of authenticity

Playa Blanca

Look
There stands
the purest vision
of infinity.
The sands of time
resting quietly
under sands of eternity.
Cycling trivialities
Above and below
Gaseous blooms
lighting the night
with their blossoms.
Born of tiny particles
Attracted
Interacted
Connected
Universal links between mortal stars.

Row Roe R'oh

Wandering in the lower field,
I found myself in a living dream

    where everything is what it seems.

Four years old, neigh forty,
and there I played in a moment

    displaced from time.

I picnicked with a cottontail
and twirled with a swallowtail

    childlike without fail.

My blurry eyes watched the skies
and The Hunter's Belt shined

    embossed at night.

Ursas dipped into the pond and scooped
droplets of hope into my cup

    a chalice filled.

I am a self-propelled boat in still waters,
pushing ripples from my center

   a sphere of influence.

I forged a wet wood fire for forty-two minutes,
until the warmth finally dried my face

   a worn embrace.

UFO traffic glanced my earthly experience
and danced in a time warp from east to west

Here I am. Now, where am I?

   a jest.

Lulled into a trance of firelight and starshine,
I surfed a new moon shrouded in mystery

   a new peace of history.

The sun peaking over the trees after
a night's worth of comfort on the rocks

   a bedroom with no locks.

There's More

Codec dreams
Or Hollywood themes
Don't touch
What I witnessed

Dark womb
With no stars
I walk the tunnel
Forward in trust

Think of a walk
And it's a flight
Of no consequence
There is here, vice versa

All is well
Be still and know
Peace within
And peace without

Loving kindness
In every moment
For beauty is love
And nature is beautiful

I am complete now
Because it was over
And mortality's will
Is last to go

I felt my movie reel
Pass through past
Experiences
Of impact

Clear to move on
Discard, draw again
Next hand dealt
New die tossed

There's always more
To perceive
To study
To heal

Conversational words
Irrelevantly lost
To instantaneous
Understandings

I agree to be here
To stay
For love
And beauty

I nod yes
Because
There is more work
To be done

There is more
There is more
There is more
There is more

Healing work
To be done
To be shone
To be honed

Shining a beacon
From shore no more
Follow my voice
Into the depth

Healing through sound
Weaving through waves
Channel flowing through
Ancient passages and causeways

There's more... so much more.